MW01248403

Kim Kiyingi is a distinguished HR and Learning & Development expert in the UAE. With over 14 years of professional experience, he has excelled in developing comprehensive training programmes, managing high-performance teams, and championing innovative learning practices. Kim's expertise also extends to delivering influential guest lectures and keynote speeches at universities in the UAE and abroad, offering valuable industry insights to students and faculty alike. Additionally, he has mentored numerous individuals worldwide, aiding their navigation through their professional journeys. His proficiency in human resources, complemented by his unique insights from diverse cultural contexts, positions him as a highly respected figure in his field. Kim channels his wealth of knowledge and experience into his book, *From Campus to Career: How to Find and Succeed in an Internship Anywhere in the World*, guiding readers through the transition from academic life to a rewarding professional career.

Successful internships yield successful career opportunities.

To you, the reader of this book
who wants to
take your internship to the next level
and even succeed at your first job.

Kim Kiyingi

FROM CAMPUS TO CAREER: HOW TO FIND AND SUCCEED IN AN INTERNSHIP ANYWHERE IN THE WORLD

AUSTIN MACAULEY PUBLISHERS™

LONDON • CAMBRIDGE • NEW YORK • SHARJAH

ISBN – 9789948746928 – (Paperback)
ISBN – 9789948746935 – (E-Book)

Application Number: MC-10-01-4406444
Age Classification: E

First Published 2024
AUSTIN MACAULEY PUBLISHERS FZE
Sharjah Publishing City
P.O Box [519201]
Sharjah, UAE
www.austinmacauley.ae
+971 655 95 202

To my dearest mother,

Since your passing in October 2023, each day has unfolded in the shadow of your absence. Yet, in the quiet moments, I feel your presence guiding me, a gentle yet profound influence that continues to shape my life. This book is more than a collection of pages; it is a tribute to the love, strength, and wisdom you imparted.

You were not just the nurturer of my early dreams but also the silent force behind my accomplishments. Your unwavering belief in me, even in moments of self-doubt, fueled my journey through the intricate world of human resources. As I rose to the role of director, your principles became my guiding light, teaching me that the heart of leadership lies in compassion and integrity.

In your modest and loving way, you taught me to see the potential in everyone, a lesson that has become the cornerstone of my professional ethos. Your insights, often shared over simple evening conversations, have been the invisible hand leading me through complex decisions and challenging moments.

This book, a reflection of my professional journey, is imbued with your spirit and wisdom. Though you are not here to share in this moment, every achievement it represents is a testament to your enduring influence.

In loving memory of the most extraordinary woman, whose legacy continues to inspire and guide me – my mother, my mentor, my forever guiding star.

With eternal love and gratitude.

Introduction

Internships are an exceptional opportunity for individuals to acquire practical experience and enhance their curriculum vitae as they shift from the academic environment to the corporate world. These programs offer a hands-on approach to learning, allowing interns to apply their theoretical knowledge to real-world situations. By participating in internships, individuals can gain a deeper understanding of their chosen field, develop their professional skills, and establish valuable connections with If you're seeking to make a mark in the professional world, whether it's by joining a well-established corporation, a budding startup, or even launching your entrepreneurial venture, securing and excelling in an internship can be a game-changer.

Participating in an internship program can be a game-changing experience for your career. It offers a unique chance to delve into the industry and gain knowledge and insights that can be invaluable in your professional journey. By going on this adventure, you will not only gain essential skills that are in great demand by businesses, but you will also learn about yourself, but also hone your critical thinking abilities to a level that will set you apart from the rest. The skills you will gain are applicable not only in your professional life but also in your personal life, as they will enable you to navigate complex situations quickly and confidently. So, take the leap and invest in yourself by developing these invaluable skills that will undoubtedly propel you toward success; however, you will have the opportunity to know more people at the organization.

By immersing yourself in the day-to-day, the platform in question presents an ideal opportunity to exhibit your unique skills and talents. It is an excellent platform to demonstrate your proficiency and expertise in a particular field. With its vast reach and diverse audience, this platform offers a remarkable chance to showcase your abilities to a broader audience and gain recognition for your hard work and dedication. So, this book is the perfect place to start if you want to make a mark in your chosen field.

In this book, *From Campus to Career: How to Find and Succeed in an Internship Anywhere in the World,* we'll explore the world of internships and help you understand their many benefits. This book offers a comprehensive guide to achieving success in an internship environment, which is a necessary step in the professional development of many college students and recent graduates. Many college students and new graduates view internships as essential for professional success.

This handbook is a humorous and straightforward guide that will lead you step-by-step through finding, applying for, and completing an internship. It is common knowledge that internships are quite nerve-racking experiences. This book provides practical tips about everything you need to know about internships. The information the intern obtains here from someone who has been there before can aid them in pursuing career advancement.

Case study; Sheila's journey: A shining example of goal-setting and career success

In personal and professional development, Sheila's journey is an excellent example of how the SMART formula can transform aspirations into achievements. Sheila not her real name. She embarked on her internship at Company SP, a digital marketing powerhouse in Dubai, and applied the art of setting SMART goals for career success. As Sheila entered the doors of Company SP, she carried with her a clear vision of what she wanted to accomplish during her internship. Using the SMART formula as her guide, she crafted Specific, Measurable, Achievable, Relevant, and Time-bound goals. When she was asked to work on a project that would benefit her company, and she needed to present it to her internship supervisor at the end of the first quarter of her internship, here is how she did it.

After identifying the company's social media pages as one area that could be improved and she had skills to help with that, Sheila's first step was to make her goals specific. Rather than simply aiming to improve the company's social media presence, she honed in on increasing the number of followers and engagement on the top social media page. Sheila set herself up for focused action and transparent progress tracking by pinpointing a specific outcome.

To ensure that her goals were measurable, Sheila established concrete metrics to track her progress. She monitored the growth in followers and analyzed engagement metrics, such as likes, comments, and shares. This allowed her to tangibly gauge the impact of her efforts and make data-driven adjustments along the way.

While aiming high, Sheila ensured her goals were Achievable. She conducted thorough market research, analyzed competitor strategies, and gained insights into industry trends. Armed with this knowledge, she set realistic targets that pushed her outside her comfort zone while remaining within the realm of possibility.

Sheila understood the importance of setting relevant goals aligned with her aspirations and the company's objectives. She took the time to understand the organization's digital marketing strategy and identified areas where her efforts could contribute significantly. By choosing goals relevant to her role and the company's success, Sheila positioned herself as a valuable asset to the team.

Lastly, Sheila infused her goals with a time-bound element. She set a timeline for achieving specific milestones, breaking her larger goal into manageable chunks. This ensured she stayed focused, maintained a sense of urgency, and celebrated small wins. Throughout her internship, Sheila's SMART goal-setting approach guided her every move. By setting Specific, Measurable, Achievable, Relevant, and Time-bound goals, she propelled herself toward success.

Sheila regularly monitored her progress, sought feedback, and adjusted her strategies when necessary. With each milestone reached, her confidence grew, and her skills sharpened. Her dedication and expertise earned her recognition and praise from her supervisor and colleagues at the end of her first quarter.

But Sheila's story didn't end there. Inspired by her exceptional performance, Company SP offered her a full-time position as an e-commerce manager. Sheila's SMART goals had not only propelled her internship success but had paved the way for a promising career.

As you embark on your journey, remember Sheila's story. Embrace the power of SMART goal-setting. Be specific about what you want to achieve, ensure your goals are Measurable, Achievable, and Relevant, and set a time-bound framework for success. With this approach, you can transform your aspirations into tangible accomplishments. Let Sheila's story motivate you to embrace personal and professional growth. Dare to dream big, take strategic action, and watch as your goals become stepping stones to a successful career. Your journey awaits, so embrace the SMART Tips in this book and let your ambitions soar.

Chapter One

We will discuss why internships are a vital stage in your career progression, as well as how this book can assist you in locating and thriving in an internship that is aligned with your aspirations and objectives. This book will provide essential insights and practical advice to help you achieve your career objectives; the choices for your future are limitless, regardless of whether you're about to graduate from high school, are starting your first year of college, whether you're an experienced expert seeking a different professional trajectory.

Whatever stage you may be on your journey in planning your next career move, there are plenty of options, and the world is your big door to career greatness. You can accomplish your objectives and scale new heights if you put in the necessary effort, commitment, and willingness to learn. The sky is the limit, don't be scared to follow your ambitions and take that leap of faith.

Being a dependable team member who maintains a professional demeanor is one of the essential things an intern can do to position themselves well for future success. This not only helps you establish a positive reputation, but it also demonstrates to your superiors and coworkers that you are focused and committed to the work that you do. Here's a list of things a student can do to become more responsible and professional:

- Arrive on time: Punctuality is essential, especially during an internship. Every day during your training, make it a point to show there on time, and if you think you might be running late or won't be able to make it, communicate this to your supervisor as soon as possible.

- Wear appropriate clothing: Your look is essential, mainly if you work an internship. Dress in a manner that fits the culture of the firm while still maintaining a professional appearance. If you are unclear about what to dress, you could either inquire with your manager or take note of what your coworkers are wearing.

- Always maintain a professional and polite demeanor. This includes showing respect to your superiors, coworkers, and customers. This includes speaking appropriately, listening carefully, and displaying gracious behavior.

- As an intern, you may be assigned duties and projects to accomplish. Thus, it would help if you took responsibility for your work. It is essential to take responsibility for your task and see it through to its conclusion. This entails not missing deadlines, seeing projects through to the end, and asking for assistance if required.

- Communicate efficiently: strong communication skills are necessary to be a competent and dependable intern. This requires you to communicate in a way that is both clear and concise, and it also requires you to respond quickly to emails and other forms of communication. Always ask questions to understand more, demonstrating your involvement in the material and eagerness to gain knowledge.

- Maintain a flexible mindset: Internships throw curveballs occasionally, and you never know when you'll be asked to take on new responsibilities or tasks.
- Maintain an attitude open to taking on new challenges and adaptable and flexible in how it approaches problems. This will demonstrate to your superiors that you can take on new responsibilities while working well within a team environment.

Keeping the above in mind, initiate the feedback conversation and be willing to accept it, whether developmental or praise: If you want to improve your work, don't be scared to ask for comments. This can assist you in recognizing areas in which you could enhance and contribute to your overall professional development. You should approach feedback with an open mind and try to apply this feedback right away so that you can also see improvements.

In summary, following the above guidelines can make you a responsible and trustworthy intern while getting the most out of your internship experience. Remember that your internship is a learning opportunity. It's your first window into the job market, taking the initiative and remaining focused on your goals. You may establish a strong foundation for a successful career in the future by doing well in your internship if you put in the effort and stay committed.

Chapter Two

This chapter will discuss an internship and why you should consider taking one locally or abroad. They're different kinds of work experience programs that are out there and the benefits that come along with them. These benefits include acquiring practical experience, cultivating professional relationships, and learning new skills. I will also guide you about how important it is to find the right internship that aligns with your career aspirations and how such an internship can influence future job opportunities.

Exploring Internships: Local and Abroad, internships are now considered an essential component of a student's path toward a prosperous and fulfilling professional future. This chapter's objective is to provide a complete understanding of internships and the significance of having one, regardless of whether the internship was completed domestically or internationally. You will receive vital insights into the prospects ahead of them if they investigate the advantages and disadvantages of both types of internships and the primary factors that should be considered.

An Explanation of Internships: Internships are structured learning experiences that allow students to apply the skills and knowledge they have gained in the classroom to a real-world situation. They give participants a chance to improve their practical skills, expand their professional networks, and investigate a variety of new career avenues. Internships provide an opportunity for personal and professional development, regardless of whether they are completed domestically or internationally.

Local internships provide several benefits, which is why it is beneficial to participate in them. To begin, they offer the advantage of working in an already familiar atmosphere to the employee, which helps to alleviate some of the stress connected with moving. In addition, local internships provide you with the opportunity to build relationships within the community and make use of the resources that are available there. For instance, gaining experience as an intern at a local business or organization may pave the way for future employment opportunities or beneficial mentoring relationships. Internships abroad offer numerous advantages.

Interning in another country provides numerous advantages that can significantly contribute to personal and professional growth. You can develop your ability to interact effectively with people of other cultures and expand your worldview by immersing yourself in another culture. You will obtain a deeper awareness of global dynamics, adaptability, and cross-cultural communication skills, which employers highly appreciate in today's globalized world due to the increased interconnectedness of the world's economies, societies, and political systems. When contemplating the possibility of participating in a local internship, evaluating the breadth of the organization's operations and its standing in the community is vital.

Do some research on the values of the organization, the work culture, and the responsibilities that will be given to you. In addition, investigate the possibilities for personal development and professional enhancement, and make sure that the internship is congruent with your long-term objectives. In addition to these factors, it is essential to consider how far you have to commute, how flexible your schedule is, and how much money you have available.

Internships Abroad: Some Considerations: Training overseas involves careful planning and consideration. To get started, research the culture, language, and work practices of the country you will be visiting. Search for internship programs or organizations with a solid reputation and can offer structured help and direction. Think about the cost of living, the procedures for getting a visa, and any vaccines that could be required. Before beginning an internship overseas, it is essential to ensure that one is well-prepared and up-to-date on relevant information.

Overcoming Obstacles: Internships at home and abroad present their respective applicants with their fair share of obstacles. Local internships may not provide the same level of exposure to various cultures and work contexts as those offered by overseas experiences. On the other hand, interning overseas may include overcoming language obstacles, experiencing homesickness, and adjusting to new cultural norms. You can successfully handle these challenges and maximize your internship experience if you acknowledge them and prepare for them in advance.

Funding Opportunities: When looking into possible internships, money issues are bound to arise, particularly if you want to pursue an overseas opportunity. Nevertheless, there are numerous alternatives for financial support. Scholarships and other forms of financial assistance can help reduce some of the strain of paying for college. In addition, some companies that offer internships will pay stipends or other forms of income to help cover living costs. Conducting research on these opportunities and submitting applications for them can make it easier to obtain internships.

To get the most out of your internship, it is essential to regularly reflect on the things you have learned and the experiences you have gained. Maintaining a journal is a great way to look back on your life and see how far you've come, professionally and personally. You can draw valuable conclusions and takeaways from your internship experience, which will help you decide about your future professional path as you reflect on the occasion. It can also help you communicate your experiences during job interviews and when revising your resume.

Conclusion: Students can improve their employability, extend their professional networks, and get significant hands-on experience by participating in internships, whether those internships are held in their home communities or other countries. Students can make informed judgements congruent with their personal and professional goals if they consider the various rewards, challenges, and essential factors involved with the two distinct types of internships. It is possible to shape their future success by taking advantage of opportunities in their immediate environment or exploring new cultural and professional contexts in other countries.

While you think about whether to take a local or international internship, think about the questions below:

- What are the goals of participating in an internship?
- How exactly will you gain from participating in local internships?

- What are the benefits of doing an internship in a foreign country?
- Before deciding on a local internship, what aspects of the position should you consider?
- What things should you be ready for before going on an internship overseas?
- What are some of the possible difficulties associated with local internships?
- What strategies can you utilize to overcome difficult times during an internship overseas?
- Where may potential interns find ways to receive financial support?
- Why is it vital to reflect while one is participating in an internship?
- Are there any books that you may recommend for further reading about internships?

Chapter Three

Internships are an excellent opportunity to obtain work experience while gaining knowledge about a specific business. Speaking from experience, before you start your internship, or earlier on, it is vital to set clear objectives for the internship. Having well-defined goals can assist you in being focused and motivated throughout your internship. Whether or not you have decided to go for a local or international internship, in this chapter, we will look at helpful hints for defining practical internship goals, taking the initiative as an intern, and how doing so can lead to fantastic chances.

A brief introduction to the goals of the internship

Internship objectives are the aims and goals you intend to accomplish during your training. These goals can be as straightforward as gaining knowledge about a particular sector or as intricate as conceiving a brand-new product or service to meet a market need. The most important thing is to devise attainable, measurable, and realistic targets.

It is possible to establish internship goals before, during, or after the internship; however, reviewing and modifying them frequently is essential to ensure that they continue to fit your overall aims.

Why do you need goals for your internship?

The goals you set for your internship are crucial because they give you a sense of where you're, where you want to go and what you will get from the work experience. These goals make it possible for you to keep your attention on the activities that need to be completed and assist you in monitoring your level of advancement. Having clearly defined goals helps you recognize areas where you shine and areas with room for improvement.

Establishing goals for your internship will also ensure you gain the most experience from it. The knowledge gained enables you to learn more about the sector of your choice and obtain experience that can be invaluable. It also allows future employers to see you, your dedication and focus on your work.

Knowing why you're doing an internship in the first place is crucial.

The internship objectives you set should allow you to monitor your development and ensure you get the most out of your internship experience. The objectives of an internship must be defined clearly, quantified, and within reach.

When deciding what you want to get from your internship, you should think about the skills you want to acquire, the projects you'd like to work on, and your overall aims for the position. The time you can devote to the internship and the materials at your disposal are essential factors to consider.

Developing Objectives for a SMART Internship

Developing SMART internship goals, which are specific, measurable, attainable, relevant, and time-bound, is vital in establishing practical goals. Effective goal-setting requires using the SMART framework, which can help direct your attention to the tasks.

When setting SMART objectives for yourself, think about the skills you want to develop, the tasks you'd like to prioritize, and the results you'd like to see. It would help to consider the energy and time you have to commit to the internship and the available resources.

The Importance of Setting Measurable Goals for the Internship

Establishing measurable goals is the next crucial step after determining your SMART objectives. Goals that can be measured are much easier to track and validate that you are progressing on the right path. Objectives that can be measured ought to be detailed and straightforward to keep tabs on. Some examples of quantifiable goals include achieving a given number of clients, completing a project within a predetermined amount of time, or growing website traffic by a particular percentage.

Check to see that your goals for the internship are in line with the overarching objectives of the program. But also, don't forget that internships can be challenging; keep the following questions in mind for a thorough internship evaluation:

- Can I achieve these objectives?
- Are the goals I've set for myself compatible with the overarching aims of the internship?
- Is the industry we're in and the company we work for related to my goals?

- Have I made any headway in accomplishing what I set out to do?
- How can I increase the likelihood of successfully achieving my objectives?
- How to overcome the most common internship challenges?

The following are some suggestions for addressing specific difficulties:

- The achievement of challenging goals can be simplified by breaking them down into more manageable subtasks.
- Inquire for assistance and direction from your peers, mentors, and bosses.
- Setting goals and time limits for your job will help you stay focused and motivated.
- Spend time thinking about how far you've come and how you may change your goals accordingly.
- Honor your achievements, but don't let them hinder your growth.

Examples of SMART goals that result in a successful internship

- **Technology Industry:** Specific: Develop proficiency in Python programming language. Measurable: Complete at least three Python projects and receive positive feedback from the team. Achievable: Attend online Python tutorials and allocate dedicated time for practice every day. Relevant: Enhance my programming skills to contribute effectively to the development team. Time-bound: Attain Python certification within three months of the internship.

- **Marketing Industry:** Specific: Gain practical experience in digital marketing strategies. Measurable: Create and implement two social media campaigns, increasing engagement by 20%. Achievable: Participate in digital marketing workshops and collaborate with the marketing team on projects. Relevant: Acquire skills in online advertising to support the company's marketing efforts. Time-bound: Present a comprehensive digital marketing plan within six weeks of starting the internship.

- **Finance Industry:** Specific: Understand the fundamentals of financial analysis. Measurable: Analyze and interpret financial statements for three different companies accurately. Achievable: Attend training sessions on economic analysis and shadow senior analysts during the internship. Relevant: Acquire knowledge in financial analysis to contribute to investment decision-making. Time-bound: Complete a comprehensive financial analysis report within two months of the training.

- **Healthcare Industry:** Specific: Develop practical communication skills with patients and healthcare professionals. Measurable: Conduct successful patient interviews and receive positive feedback from the healthcare team. Achievable: Participate in patient communication workshops and engage in role-playing exercises. Relevant: Improve patient care by establishing empathetic and clear communication. Time-bound: Demonstrate proficient communication skills within the first month of the internship.

- **Fashion Industry:** Specific: Learn the fashion design process from concept to production. Measurable: Create a fashion design portfolio with at least five original designs. Achievable: Assist the design team in various stages of the design process and attend fashion events. Relevant: Develop a strong foundation in fashion design to pursue a career in the industry. Time-bound: Complete the fashion design portfolio within three months of the internship.

- **Hospitality Industry:** Specific: Enhance customer service skills and knowledge in the hospitality sector. Measurable: Receive positive feedback from guests through customer satisfaction surveys, with a target of 90% satisfaction rating. Achievable: Attend customer service training sessions, shadow experienced staff, and seek feedback to improve performance. Relevant: Provide exceptional service to guests, ensuring a positive and memorable experience. Time-bound: Achieve the target satisfaction rating within three months of the internship.

- **Engineering Industry:** Specific: Develop proficiency in AutoCAD software for engineering design. Measurable: Complete at least two engineering design projects using AutoCAD, with positive feedback from the engineering team.

27

Achievable: Attend AutoCAD training sessions, practice regularly, and collaborate with senior engineers on design assignments. Relevant: Acquire essential skills in engineering design software to contribute effectively to future projects. Time-bound: Complete the two engineering design projects using AutoCAD within four months of the internship.

- **Tourism Industry**: Specific: Improve destination management and customer service knowledge and skills. Measurable: Receive positive feedback from tourists through surveys, with a target of 95% satisfaction rating. Achievable: Attend destination management workshops, engage with tourists, and seek guidance from experienced professionals. Relevant: Enhance the ability to create exceptional travel experiences and promote tourism destinations. Time-bound: Achieve the target satisfaction rating within three months of the internship.

- **Education: Specific:** Develop practical classroom management skills. Measurable: Implement classroom management strategies and maintain a positive learning environment, evidenced by improved student engagement and discipline. Achievable: Attend workshops on classroom management techniques, observe experienced teachers, and seek feedback from mentors. Relevant: Enhance the ability to create an optimal learning environment for students. Time-bound: Demonstrate improved classroom management within the first month of the internship.

- **Law: Specific:** Gain practical experience in legal research and writing. Measurable: Prepare at least three comprehensive legal briefs with accurate analysis and citations. Achievable: Shadow experienced attorneys, attend legal writing workshops, and actively participate in research projects. Relevant: Develop legal research and writing skills to support future legal practice. Time-bound: Complete the three legal briefs within four months of the internship.

- **Community Development:** Specific: Contribute to developing a community outreach program. Measurable: Successfully organize and execute at least two community events or initiatives, impacting many individuals. Achievable: Collaborate with community leaders, participate in planning meetings, and actively engage with community members. Relevant: Contribute to the improvement and well-being of the community through effective initiatives. Time-bound: Organize and execute the two community events within six months of the internship.

- **Volunteering: Specific:** Develop leadership and teamwork skills in a volunteer setting. Measurable: Successfully led a team of volunteers in executing a project, receiving positive feedback from the team and project beneficiaries. Achievable: Take on leadership roles within volunteer projects, attend leadership development workshops, and actively seek opportunities to collaborate with fellow volunteers. Relevant: Enhance leadership and teamwork abilities to impact volunteer initiatives positively. Time-bound: Demonstrate effective leadership and teamwork within the first three months of the internship.

Remember, SMART goals are Specific, Measurable, Achievable, Relevant, and Time-bound, providing a clear framework for success and personal growth during an internship. It is necessary to assess them consistently. Checking in on your goals frequently ensures you are progressing in the right direction. One of the musts for any internship, make a list of realistic goals for the time you spend there. It helps you maintain concentration, stay motivated, and stay on track. Additionally, it assists you in measuring your progress and identifying areas in which you may improve.

The Advantages of Showing Initiative While Working as an Intern

As an intern, taking the initiative can be a terrific way to stand out and create a positive impression on your supervisor. Taking the industry demonstrates that you are proactive and willing to undertake new obligations and duties. Additionally, it might assist you in learning more about the sector and gaining experience, both of which are extremely valuable.

How to Show Initiative When Working as an Intern

As an intern, taking the initiative demands you to be proactive and eager to take on additional chores and responsibilities. You must also be willing to learn new skills.

The list below includes a few suggestions that can help you as an intern to take the initiative:

- Make yourself heard and ask questions.
- Accept additional responsibility and expand your scope of work.
- Give your coworkers the benefit of your support and assistance.
- Inquire about comments and consider how to apply them constructively.
- Make an effort to undertake new initiatives on your initiative.
- Putting fresh ideas and solutions into action.
- Volunteer offer to assist with a task or project.
- Taking responsibility is a step in the right direction.
- Pointing out problem areas and offering potential solutions.
- Participating in the role of a mentor for other interns.

The great chances that can be created simply by taking the initiative an intern can open the door to a world of beautiful opportunities. It can help you stand out and leave a positive impression on your superiors and coworkers. Additionally, it might assist you in learning more about the sector and gaining experience, both of which are extremely valuable.

Taking the initiative often results in favorable outcomes in one's professional life. It demonstrates to prospective employers that you are proactive, motivated, and willing to take on new duties and tasks.

Conclusion

As an intern, taking the initiative can be a terrific way to stand out and create a positive impression on your supervisor. Additionally, it might help you learn more about the sector and obtain essential experience while opening the door to fantastic prospects. You must be proactive, driven, and willing to take on new duties and tasks to take the initiative. If you have the correct abilities and mentality, you can show initiative and leave a positive impression on others.

Chapter Four

The measures that you need to follow to get ready for an internship will be covered in this chapter. To locate possible internship opportunities, I will discuss researching organizations and industries, developing an impressive résumé and professional internet presence, and engaging in professional networking. I will give you advice and resources to set you apart from competitors and put you in a better position to succeed.

So, whether it's a local or international internship, congratulations on embarking on your internship journey! As you navigate the exciting world of professional development, expanding your professional network is one aspect that holds immense potential for your future success. This chapter will explore the most effective ways to build meaningful connections, create lasting relationships, and open doors to new opportunities while interning. We will uncover the secrets to networking success through engaging examples and real-life scenarios, ensuring you stay captivated throughout your journey.

Maximizing Networking Opportunities

Attend Networking Events: Seize the Moment

Imagine yourself at an industry conference, surrounded by professionals who share your passion. Engaging in conversations and making genuine connections can open doors to exciting opportunities. Attend meetings, professional meetups, and company-sponsored events relevant to your field. For instance, while interning at a marketing agency, I attend marketing summits to meet industry experts, gain insights, and forge valuable connections.

Engage with Colleagues and Mentors: Forge Relationships

Your colleagues and mentors are invaluable resources for guidance and support. Seek their advice, share your ideas, and offer assistance whenever possible. Building rapport and trust can lead to lasting connections. For example, contact senior colleagues for coffee chats to learn about their career paths, seek advice on your professional journey, and develop a strong support network.

Leveraging Digital Platforms

Utilize Social Media Platforms: Connect and Engage

Harness the power of social media to expand your network. LinkedIn is an excellent platform for connecting with professionals, joining industry groups, and sharing internship experiences. Engage in X discussions, participate in relevant hashtags (formerly known as Twitter, and showcase your industry knowledge. Even Instagram can be used creatively to highlight your internship journey, giving potential connections a glimpse into your professional growth.

Tapping into Professional Communities

Join Professional Associations: Find Your Tribe

Professional associations and industry-specific organizations offer a goldmine of networking opportunities.

Seek out local chapters or student associations aligned with your field of interest. Attend their events, discuss, and connect with like-minded individuals who can become valuable contacts throughout your career. For instance, join the Young Entrepreneurs Association or the Women in Tech Society to connect with professionals who share your aspirations.

Going Above and Beyond

Volunteer for Extra Projects: Expand Your Horizons

Take the initiative to contribute beyond your assigned tasks—volunteer for additional projects that allow you to collaborate with different teams and gain exposure to diverse professionals. By showcasing your dedication and skills, you leave a lasting impression and create networking opportunities. For example, as we saw in the earlier chapter, offer to assist a senior colleague with a challenging project or contribute your expertise to a cross-functional team like Sheila did to achieve her success.

Nurturing Connections for the Future

Conduct Informational Interviews: Learn and Connect

Reach out to professionals whose career paths inspire you and request informational interviews. These interviews offer a chance to gain insights, learn about different industries, and build relationships that can be nurtured for future opportunities. For instance, connect with a marketing manager in a company you admire and explore their experiences, challenges, and advice for aspiring professionals.

Attend Company-sponsored Workshops: Develop Your Skills

Participating in workshops and development programs organized by your company demonstrates your commitment to growth. These initiatives provide opportunities to network with colleagues from various departments and showcase your dedication to personal and professional development. For example, enroll in leadership development workshops or cross-functional training sessions to expand your skill set and connect with professionals across different teams.

Building a Supportive Internship Community

Participate in Internship Programs or Clubs: Collaborate and Share

Engage with your fellow interns by participating in internship programs or clubs offered by your company. Collaborate on projects, share experiences and resources, and build a supportive network within your intern community. For instance, join an intern committee focused on community engagement, where you can work together on volunteer initiatives and foster meaningful connections.

Seek Mentorship Opportunities: Learn from the Best

Identify experienced professionals within your organization or industry and establish mentor-mentee relationships. Seek their guidance, leverage their insights, and learn from their experiences. Mentors can provide valuable advice, open doors to new opportunities, and help shape your career trajectory. For example, connect with a senior executive who can offer guidance on navigating the corporate landscape and provide career advice tailored to your aspirations.

Nurturing Connections for Long-term Success

Follow Up and Stay Connected: Maintain Relationships

After networking events, informational interviews, or mentorship meetings, send personalized thank-you notes to express your gratitude and demonstrate your professionalism. Stay in touch with your connections through email or LinkedIn, sharing relevant industry articles, congratulating them on their achievements, or simply checking in on their professional journey. Attend reunions or alums events to reconnect with previous colleagues and expand your network further.

You now possess the tools to expand your professional network and create lasting connections during your internship. By attending networking events, engaging with colleagues and mentors, leveraging social media, joining professional associations, volunteering for extra projects, conducting informational interviews, attending workshops, participating in internship programs or clubs, seeking mentorship opportunities, and nurturing connections, you are well-equipped to unlock doors to future opportunities and ignite your career growth.

Embrace the power of networking, cultivate meaningful relationships, and seize the potential within your network. Your internship experience will be transformative, personally and professionally, and the connections you build will stay with you throughout your career.

Chapter Five

Now, it's time to make the most of this opportunity by actively seeking feedback and leveraging it to ensure a successful internship experience. This chapter will explore the importance of intern feedback, how to request it, and strategies for handling constructive criticism.

We will also delve into the best practices for seeking feedback, engaging with colleagues, and using it to enhance your professional growth. Throughout this chapter, I'll keep you involved with original examples, a list of websites to locate internship opportunities and college resources. So, let's dive in and unlock the power of feedback to make the most of your internship!

The Value of Intern Feedback

Understanding Intern Feedback: Fuel for Growth

Intern feedback refers to receiving and seeking feedback on your performance from superiors and colleagues during your internship. It is an invaluable tool for personal growth, helping you identify areas of improvement and where you excel. By embracing feedback, you can better understand your role, the company's culture, and the industry. Feedback also allows you to build relationships with peers and supervisors, improve communication skills, and enrich your professional portfolio.

Embracing Constructive Criticism: The Key to Growth

Receiving negative feedback can be challenging, but it's essential to approach it with an open and honest mindset. Constructive criticism provides valuable insights that can help you become a better intern and a more competent employee overall. Remember, it's not a reflection of your worth as an individual but an opportunity for growth. By being receptive to feedback and using it to your advantage, you can position yourself for future success.

Strategies for Seeking Intern Feedback

Making Specific Requests: Asking the Right Questions

When seeking feedback, asking specific questions addressing the areas you want to improve is crucial. For instance, you can request feedback on your communication skills, teamwork abilities, problem-solving approach, time management, and professional conduct. By making targeted inquiries, you enable others to provide meaningful feedback tailored to your development needs.

Approaching Others for Feedback: Building Connections and Gaining Insights

During your internship, seeking feedback from others can be a valuable opportunity for growth. Approaching someone for feedback requires a thoughtful approach and effective communication. Here are some strategies to consider:

- Choose the Right Moment: Find a suitable time when the person you want to approach is available and not occupied with pressing tasks. It's best to avoid interrupting someone during a busy period or an important project.

- Express Appreciation: Begin the conversation by expressing gratitude for their time and willingness to provide feedback. Please acknowledge that you value their insights, and their input will contribute to your professional development.
- Be Specific: Communicate the areas in which you would like feedback. You guide the person toward offering relevant and actionable insights by being specific. For example, in a recent project, you can ask for feedback on your communication skills during team meetings or your problem-solving approach.
- Encourage Honesty: Emphasize that you are open to constructive criticism and genuinely interested in improving. Assure them that their honest feedback will be appreciated and taken constructively. This helps create a safe space for open and honest communication.
- Active Listening: While receiving feedback, actively listen to what the person says. Maintain eye contact, a nod to show understanding, and ask clarifying questions. This demonstrates your attentiveness and willingness to learn from their perspective.

Sample Questions for Seeking Intern Feedback

When approaching someone for feedback, asking the right questions can guide the conversation toward valuable insights. Here are some examples of questions you can ask:

- How do you perceive my communication skills within the team? Are there any areas where I could improve?
- Can you provide feedback on my teamwork abilities? Is there anything I could do differently to collaborate more effectively?
- In problem-solving, are there any specific areas where you feel I excel? Are there any suggestions for improvement?
- How would you assess my time management skills? Are there any strategies you recommend to enhance my efficiency?
- From your observations, how would you evaluate my professional conduct and ability to adapt to the workplace environment?

Timing and Gratitude: Keys to Successful Feedback Requests

Timing is crucial when soliciting feedback. Try to ask for feedback soon after completing a project or assignment to ensure it's fresh in everyone's mind. Express your gratitude to those who provide feedback and show appreciation for their time and insights. A simple thank-you note or an in-person acknowledgement can go a long way in fostering a positive feedback culture.

Leveraging Feedback for Growth

Processing Feedback: Listening and Reflecting

When receiving feedback, actively listen to the comments and suggestions offered. Avoid taking criticism personally and maintain a receptive attitude toward improvement. Take time to reflect on the feedback before responding, allowing yourself to digest the information and consider how it aligns with your professional goals.

Following Up and Taking Action: Transforming Feedback into Results

After receiving feedback, following up with your colleagues to discuss further questions or seek clarification is essential. Use the feedback to identify areas for improvement and create an action plan to address them. Seek guidance and assistance from others when necessary, and monitor your progress as you implement the necessary changes.

Section 4: Maximizing College Resources and Online Platforms

Utilizing College Resources: Unlocking Internship Opportunities

Your college can be a valuable resource for finding internship opportunities. Explore the career services department, attend job fairs, and participate in networking events your college hosts. College-specific online platforms, such as alum networks and job boards, can provide access to internships tailored to your interest.

Online Platforms for Internship Opportunities: Widening Your Scope

Expand your search beyond traditional methods by exploring various online platforms specializing in internship listings. Here are some popular websites to help you locate internship opportunities:

- LinkedIn: Create a professional profile and join industry-related groups to connect with professionals and discover internships.
- Indeed: Use search filters to find internships based on location, industry, and duration.
- Glassdoor: Access internship listings, company reviews, and ratings to gain insights into the work environment.
- InternMatch: Browse through a wide range of internships across industries and locations.
- *https://www.globalexperiences.com*
- *https://www.internshiptocareer.com*
- *https://www.goabroad.com*
- *https://absoluteinternship.com*
- *https://www.internjobs.com*
- *https://erasmusintern.org*
- *https://www.gooverseas.com/internships-abroad*
- *https://www.theinterngroup.com*
- *https://worldwideinternships.org*
- *https://www.wayup.com*
- *https://www.internmatch.com/*

Making Direct Contact with Employers

Crafting Effective Email Inquiries: Introducing Yourself Professionally

Writing a well-crafted email can make a positive impression when directly contacting employers. Here's a sample structure to guide you:

Subject: Inquiry for Internship Opportunity at [Company Name]

Dear [Contact's Name],

I hope this email finds you well. My name is [Your Name], and I am a [Your Year/Major] student at [Your College/University]. I recently came across [Company Name] and was inspired by [specific reason: their innovative projects, industry reputation, company culture, etc.].

I am writing to inquire if any internship opportunities are available at [Company Name] for the upcoming [season/semester]. I am particularly interested in gaining hands-on experience in [relevant area]. I have attached my resume for your reference.

I would greatly appreciate any information or guidance you can provide regarding internship opportunities within your organization. I am eager to contribute my skills and learn from the talented professionals at [Company Name].

Thank you for considering my inquiry. I look forward to the possibility of discussing potential internship opportunities further.

Sincerely, [Your Name] [Contact Information]

You now have the knowledge and strategies to maximize feedback during your internship and actively seek growth opportunities. By embracing intern feedback, utilizing college resources, exploring online platforms, and making direct contact with employers, you can enhance your internship experience and position yourself for future success. Remember to be open to constructive criticism, express gratitude, and leverage feedback to improve continually.

Your internship journey has the potential to propel you toward your long-term professional goals, so seize every opportunity to learn, grow, and connect. Good luck with your internship adventure!

Chapter Six

The internship application process plays a crucial role in securing valuable professional experience. In this chapter, I will guide you through crafting an impressive cover letter, designing a standout resume, and excelling in the interview. Following our pointers and recommendations will elevate your application above others and increase your chances of landing the internship of your dreams.

Section 1: Writing an Effective Cover Letter

A well-written cover letter can make a significant impact on potential employers. It allows you to showcase your enthusiasm, highlight relevant skills, and demonstrate why you are the ideal candidate for the internship. Here are some critical tips for writing an effective cover letter:

- Personalize your letter: Address the recipient by their name and tailor your content to the specific internship and organization. Show that you have researched and understand their mission, values, and goals.
- Grab attention with a strong opening: Begin your letter with a captivating introduction that immediately grabs the reader's attention. Consider sharing a compelling anecdote, expressing your passion for the industry, or mentioning a specific accomplishment related to the internship.

- Highlight relevant skills and experiences: Use the body paragraphs to elaborate on your skills, experiences, and achievements that directly align with the internship requirements. Provide concrete examples to demonstrate your capabilities and how they can contribute to the organization.
- Showcase your motivation and fit: Clearly articulate why you are interested in the internship and how it aligns with your career goals. Explain how your values, interests, and skills make you an excellent fit for the organization. This shows your genuine enthusiasm and commitment.
- Close with a firm conclusion: Summarize your key points and reiterate your interest in the internship. Express gratitude for the opportunity to be considered, and include your contact information for further communication.

Designing an Impressive Resume

Your resume is a crucial tool for showcasing your abilities and expertise. A well-designed resume will highlight your relevant experiences, skills, and accomplishments clearly and concisely. Here are some tips for creating an impressive resume:

- Organize your information effectively: Structure your resume with clear sections, such as "Education," "Work Experience," "Skills," and "Achievements." Use bullet points to describe your responsibilities and accomplishments in each role concisely.

- Tailor your resume to the internship: Customize your resume to highlight the experiences and skills that directly relate to the internship position. Review the internship description and incorporate relevant keywords and phrases throughout your resume.

- Highlight your achievements: Showcase your accomplishments and contributions in previous roles. Quantify your achievements whenever possible, such as "increased sales by X%," "led a team of Y members," or "completed Z projects ahead of schedule."

- Emphasize relevant skills: Identify the critical skills required for the internship and ensure they are prominently displayed on your resume. This could include technical skills, soft skills, or specific industry-related competencies.

- Include a well-written summary or objective statement: Begin your resume with concise, accurate information that captures your career goals and highlights your strengths. This provides a quick overview for employers and encourages them to read further.

- Proofread and format meticulously: Avoid grammatical errors and typos by carefully proofreading your resume. Choose a clean and professional design, use consistent fonts and headings, and ensure the document is well-organized and easy to read.

Excelling in the Interview

Securing an interview is an exciting opportunity to showcase your skills, personality, and potential to the employer. To excel in the interview process, consider the following tips:

- Research the organization: Gain a thorough understanding of the organization's values, culture, products/services, and recent news. This knowledge will enable you to ask insightful questions and demonstrate your genuine interest in the company.

- Prepare responses to common interview questions: Anticipate and practice your answers beforehand. Be ready to provide specific examples highlighting your skills, experiences, and achievements.

- Showcase your soft skills: Besides technical competencies, employers value soft skills such as communication, teamwork, problem-solving, and adaptability. Prepare examples that demonstrate how you have utilized these skills in previous experiences.

- Ask thoughtful questions: Prepare a list of intelligent questions for the interviewer. This demonstrates your interest, engagement, and critical thinking abilities. Ask about the internship responsibilities, company culture, or recent projects or initiatives.

- Dress professionally and arrive early: Dress appropriately for the interview, aiming for a professional and polished appearance. Plan to arrive early at the interview location to allow time for unforeseen circumstances.

- Demonstrate enthusiasm and confidence: Show genuine enthusiasm for the internship and the organization. Maintain good eye contact, engage in active listening, and exhibit confidence in your abilities and potential contributions.

Example of a Well-Written Cover Letter:
[Your Name]
[Your Address]
[City, State, Postal Code]
[Email Address]
[Phone Number]
[Date]
[Recipient's Name]
[Recipient's Job Title]
[Company/Organization Name]
[Company Address]
[City, State, Postal Code]

Dear [Recipient's Name],

I am writing to express my keen interest in the [Internship Position] at [Company/Organization Name]. With my passion for [Industry/Field] and strong dedication to personal and professional growth, I am confident I can contribute to [Company/ Organization Name] and make a meaningful impact.

Having researched extensively about [Company/ Organization Name], I am impressed by your innovative approach to [specific aspect of the industry]. Your commitment to [shared value or goal] resonates with me, and I am excited about the opportunity to work alongside like-minded individuals who strive for excellence.

Throughout my academic journey at [University Name], where I am pursuing a [Degree Program], I have gained a solid foundation in [relevant skills or knowledge]. Additionally, my experiences as a [relevant experience] have honed my abilities in [specific skills]. I am particularly drawn to [particular aspect of the internship] as it aligns perfectly with my interests and aspirations.

One of my proudest accomplishments was [specific achievement or project] during my recent internship at [Company/ Organization Name]. This experience allowed me to showcase my [relevant skills] while working collaboratively with a diverse team to [specific outcome or result]. It reinforced my ability to adapt to dynamic environments, think critically, and solve complex problems.

At [Company/Organization Name], I am confident that I can contribute my skills in [relevant skills], my strong work ethic, and my passion for [industry/field]. I am eager to leverage my knowledge and gain hands-on experience in [specific tasks or responsibilities]. Furthermore, I believe my excellent communication skills, attention to detail, and ability to thrive in fast-paced environments will enable me to excel in this role.

Thank you for considering my application. I am genuinely enthusiastic about the opportunity to contribute to [Company/ Organization Name]. I would welcome the chance to discuss further how my skills and experiences align with your internship requirements. I have attached my resume for your review. Please feel free to contact me at your convenience via phone or email.

Thank you for your time and consideration.

Sincerely,
[Your Name]

Example of a Well-Designed Resume:

[Your Name] [Contact Information: Phone Number, Email Address]

Objective: A dedicated and driven [your field] student seeking an internship opportunity to apply and further develop my skills in [specific area of interest]. Eager to contribute to [company/organization] through [relevant skills] and a strong work ethic.

Education: [Bachelor's/Master's Degree], [Field of Study] [University Name], [City, State] [Dates of Attendance]

Relevant Coursework:

Skills:

- Technical Skills: [List relevant technical skills]
- Soft Skills: [List relevant soft skills]
- Languages: [List languages and proficiency levels]

Experience: [Internship/ Job Position] [Company/ Organization Name], [City, State] [Dates of Employment]

- [Responsibility/Achievement 1]: [Description of your responsibilities and accomplishments]
- [Responsibility/Achievement 2]: [Description of your duties and actions]
- [Responsibility/Achievement 3]: [Description of your responsibilities and accomplishments]

Projects:

* [Project 1]: [Description of the project and your role]
* [Project 2]: [Description of the project and your part]
* [Project 3]: [Description of the project and your role]

Leadership and Extracurricular Activities:

* [Activity 1]: [Description of your involvement and responsibilities]
* [Activity 2]: [Description of your involvement and duties]
* [Activity 3]: [Description of your involvement and responsibilities]

Certifications and Awards:

* [Certification 1]: [Description of the accreditation and issuing organization]
* [Certification 2]: [Description of the certificate and administering organization]
* [Award 1]: [Description of the award and awarding organization]

References: Available upon request

Another Case study about one of my mentees and how she navigated the challenges above.

Katerina's Journey: Triumphing over Internship Challenges

She started her internship in a bustling city, her first internship experience and an ambitious individual named Katerina. She was excited as she landed an internship at Company X, a prestigious organization in her chosen field. Katerina saw this as her chance to gain real-world experience and kickstart her career. Little did she know that the path ahead would be laden with unexpected difficulties.

As Katerina stepped into her role as an intern, she found herself confronted with a demanding workload that stretched far beyond the regular office hours. The long hours left her feeling drained and tested her ability to manage her time effectively. Determined not to be overwhelmed, Katerina realized she needed to strike a balance. She diligently prioritized her tasks, set realistic deadlines, and communicated openly with her supervisor about her workload. Taking short breaks throughout the day became her secret weapon to maintain productivity and protect her well-being.

However, Katerina's eagerness to contribute and learn hit a roadblock when she discovered that the assignments she received did not align with her career goals. Disappointment gnawed at her, but she refused to let it consume her spirit. Katerina summoned her courage and approached her supervisor, expressing her passion for more significant projects that would challenge and develop her skills. Her proactive approach caught the attention of her supervisor, who recognized her enthusiasm and gradually started assigning her tasks aligned with her aspirations.

Yet the feeling of unmet expectations was not the only hurdle Katerina faced. She yearned for recognition—the affirmation that her efforts were noticed and valued. However, there were moments when she felt invisible as if her work went unnoticed. Determined to break through this barrier, Katerina took matters into her own hands. She sought feedback from her colleagues and supervisor, engaging in open conversations about her performance and areas for improvement.

Moreover, she seized every opportunity to demonstrate her skills by actively participating in team discussions, offering insightful perspectives, and willingly taking on leadership roles whenever available. Slowly but surely, her contributions began to be recognized, and the appreciation she craved started to pour in from both colleagues and supervisors.

Through her perseverance and adaptability, Katerina triumphed over the difficulties of internships. Her journey transformed her, and became a source of inspiration for her fellow interns and colleagues. She emerged as a shining star at Company X, showcasing her unwavering dedication and positive attitude.

As the internship drew close, Katerina conquered the challenges and turned her experience into a valuable lesson in growth and resilience. Her story is a testament to the power of perseverance, proactive communication, and maintaining a positive mindset in the face of adversity. Katerina's journey continues to inspire others, reminding them that with determination and the right attitude, they can overcome the hurdles that come their way and emerge stronger than ever before.

I am delighted to share the remarkable journey of Katerina, who fearlessly tackled the challenges of her internship at Company X. Her story is truly inspiring, as she demonstrated unwavering determination, resilience, and a proactive approach, turning obstacles into opportunities for personal growth and development.

Katerina's experience offers us invaluable lessons about the intern journey. Firstly, it underscores the importance of maintaining a healthy work-life balance, even with extended hours. By prioritizing tasks, setting boundaries, and taking regular breaks, interns can safeguard their well-being and sustain their productivity.

Secondly, Katerina's journey highlights the significance of open communication and proactive initiative. Interns should express their career aspirations and seek assignments aligning with their goals. By actively engaging with supervisors and colleagues, interns can shape their internship experiences to reflect their professional interests.

Moreover, Katerina's determination to be acknowledged emphasizes the value of self-advocacy. Interns should actively seek feedback, demonstrate their skills, and contribute to team efforts. By taking ownership of their growth and consistently delivering high-quality work, interns can earn recognition for their valuable contributions.

Lastly, Katerina's triumph exemplifies the transformative power of a positive mindset. Despite facing setbacks and unmet expectations, she remained resilient, focused on her goals, and maintained an optimistic outlook throughout her internship. This mindset enabled her to persevere and turn her experience into a springboard for success.

As readers, we are invited to embrace these lessons wholeheartedly. Whether we are interns, professionals, or individuals aspiring to greatness, Katerina's story is a powerful reminder that challenges are inevitable in any journey. By adopting a proactive approach, nurturing resilience, seeking feedback, and cultivating a positive mindset, we can navigate difficulties and transform them into stepping stones toward personal and professional growth.

In conclusion, let Katerina's tale ignite your spirit. Embrace the difficulties that come with internships, for it is within these challenges that the seeds of growth and opportunity are sown. Remember that you have the power to overcome obstacles, shape your experiences, and emerge as a more assertive, accomplished individual, ready to conquer the world.

Internships provide a valuable opportunity to expand your skill set, gain professional experience, and establish meaningful connections. By following our guidance on crafting a compelling cover letter, designing an impressive resume, and excelling in interviews, you can significantly increase your chances of securing the desired internship. Remember to personalize your application materials, highlight relevant experiences and skills, and showcase your enthusiasm and dedication. With these strategies, you can maximize your internship application process and set yourself apart from other candidates.

Chapter Seven

In this chapter, I will review what you can anticipate happening during your internship. I will discuss topics such as orientation and training, developing connections with coworkers, taking the initiative and contributing to the team, and prospects for personal development and professional advancement. I will share our knowledge and offer guidance to ensure you maximize your internship experience and position yourself for future success.

The prospect of commencing an internship this year might be nerve-wracking, mainly if the internship will be carried out outside the country. Maintaining a professional demeanor at all times and being trustworthy in all you do while participating in an internship are two of the most important things you can do to ensure you get the most out of the experience.

Being dependable and acting professionally are two of the most crucial things you can do during an internship. In this chapter, we will investigate six important strategies that can be utilized to accomplish these goals. Following these rules can make a good impression on your superiors and have a more delightful experience. This will be the case, whether or not you follow these instructions.

- Make sure you're not late.

In any internship position this year, promptness is one of the most important aspects for determining one's level of success. It does not matter if you are starting a new internship or just heading in for the day; you are required to come at the time allotted for the start of your shift. This will show that you are professional and ensure you can maximize your time in the office and all the learning opportunities presented.

If you are late for work, you must notify your employer as soon as possible; doing so will show them that you value punctuality and appreciate the time they have given you. In addition, if you have to leave early for any reason, make sure that you offer as much warning as possible so that your absence does not negatively impact the team's productivity and the quality of the work you create. It would help if you arrived on time daily to ensure an excellent overall experience during your internship.

- Establish your persona through your outward look.

You should always dress correctly for the position you are interning in, which applies regardless of the type of internship you are undertaking. It is possible to estimate your professionalism level based on how you present yourself. The industry you work in and the culture of the company you work for each may have their own unique set of dress codes that employees are expected to follow. Before you start your first day at the workplace, you should research the attire expected there so that you can get dressed accordingly.

It is to one's advantage to on professionalism and conservatism in almost all cases. It would help to avoid wearing anything overly provocative or lax. In addition to that, check to see that all of your items have been ironed and that there are no wrinkles. Because of how you present yourself at work, your superiors and your coworkers will form favorable opinions of your work ethic and professionalism.

- Remain current on the most recent advancements that have been made in the industry.

It does not matter what kind of internship job you perform; staying informed about recent developments and trends is necessary. This should be kept in mind no matter what industry you work in. As an intern, you will be given a once-in-a-lifetime opportunity to get first-hand experience and industry-specific information in the field that interests you. Regular industry news reading can better understand your work's context and job demands.

Keep up with the most recent advancements by regularly reading industry-specific trade magazines, papers, websites, and social media accounts explicitly geared toward the topic. This will not only guarantee that you are well-prepared for any work that may be handed to you during your internship, but it will also help you keep up with the most recent advancements and trends in your industry.

- Take responsibility for the current predicament.

One of the most important things to remember when working as an intern is the requirement to exhibit initiative. When applying for internships, you should always put your best foot forward because these roles often act as stepping stones to more permanent opportunities later in a person's professional life. One must go above and beyond the obligations linked with their position and accept extra responsibilities whenever they are provided to display initiative.

You might even suggest taking on additional tasks or delivering solutions of great value. This demonstrates that you are willing to make the necessary effort to achieve the job successfully. When you hunt for internships in the future, doing so will also display your competence and awareness of the area, which will help you stand out among the other applicants and make you more competitive. If you do this, you will increase your chances of getting hired for the role you want.

- Refrain from indulging in any idle chatter.

Conversations with other people are inappropriate in an environment where professionalism is expected. It is essential to abstain from spreading rumors and making assumptions about other employees, especially if it is tempting to join in on the conversation while your coworkers are chatting about their internship chances, even though it may be tempting to join in on the chat. It is important to remember that spreading rumors and assumptions about other employees can have serious consequences. Maintain your standing in the professional community by avoiding conversations that involve gossip. Instead, prioritize zeroing in on the task and getting things done despite distractions.

If someone does begin a discussion about another individual, you should gently direct that person's focus to something else. It would be to your advantage to remember that whatever you put online can be linked back to you and may affect your professional life at some point in the future. You may protect your reputation and company if you refrain from participating in meaningless small talk.

- Make a positive contribution to the work that the group is doing.

Interns must be able to get along well with people and collaborate effectively. When searching for an internship, the capacity to work well in a group setting is a highly sought-after quality. Contributing to the team's success is crucial by assisting coworkers, exchanging ideas, and actively listening to their feedback. Teamwork is what makes the dream function, and it is really necessary to be able to assist the people you work with.

Regarding cooperating as a team, communication is among the most critical factors. If there is something that you are unsure of or if you require assistance, do not be afraid to ask questions about it. It would be beneficial if you could help your teammates whenever they have a question or concern. In addition, always have a positive outlook and try to positively influence the people around you, especially when things are challenging.

An intern is expected to be dependable and professional at all times; excellent ways to fulfill these requirements include taking the initiative, arriving on time, and appropriately dressing for the situation. But if you want to go above and beyond this, you need to be able to collaborate well with other people. If you can show your coworkers that you are willing to cooperate to accomplish the team's objectives, you will demonstrate that you are an integral part of the group and earn a place of prominence.

Case Study Three

Navigating the Internship Maze and Cultivating Professional Relationships

In IT innovation, Julius, a fresh-faced graduate, entered an esteemed IT firm as an intern. Little did he know that his journey would be filled with unexpected hurdles, challenging his resilience and testing his ability to forge meaningful connections. Join Julius as he learns to navigate the intricacies of the workplace and discovers the transformative power of interpersonal skills.

As Julius began his internship, he struggled to connect with his coworkers. Being a fresh graduate, he felt the weight of inexperience and questioned whether he could contribute to the team. The firm's employees, immersed in their daily routines, seemed distant and unapproachable, leaving Julius feeling isolated and unfairly treated.

Determined to turn the situation around without resigning from his internship, Julius recognized the importance of honing his interpersonal skills. He embarked on a journey of self-improvement, focusing on building connections and establishing rapport with his coworkers.

Julius understood that effective communication was vital in breaking down barriers. He actively sought opportunities to engage in professional and personal conversations with his colleagues. By asking questions, showing genuine interest, and actively listening, Julius demonstrated his eagerness to learn and his commitment to the team's success.

To further foster connections, Julius embraced the power of collaboration. He sought out projects, where he could contribute his unique perspectives and skills while also supporting his coworkers. By being a proactive team player and offering assistance whenever possible, Julius gained the trust and respect of his colleagues.

Julius's resilience and determination did not go unnoticed. Over time, his coworkers began recognizing his dedication and willingness to learn. They saw him not as a fresh graduate but a valuable team member. Julius's efforts to turn his situation around transformed the workplace dynamics, fostering a more inclusive and supportive environment.

As his internship ended, Julius emerged with newfound confidence and experience. Armed with his cultivated connections, he confidently entered his first job after completing the training.

The connections Julius had developed during his internship proved invaluable as he navigated the early stages of his career. The support and mentorship he received from his former coworkers opened doors and provided guidance. Julius's ability to adapt, connect, and collaborate helped him excel in his new role and positioned him for long-term success.

Julius's journey is a testament to the transformative power of perseverance and interpersonal skills. It serves as a reminder to all those facing similar challenges that adversity can be overcome. One can forge meaningful relationships and thrive in any professional setting by embracing the opportunity to learn and grow, actively seeking connections and demonstrating genuine interest in others.

So, dear reader, take Julius's story to heart. Embrace each challenge as an opportunity to develop your interpersonal skills and forge connections. Remember that your experience level does not determine your worth but your willingness to learn and contribute. With resilience, determination, and a commitment to cultivating professional relationships, you, too, can triumph and create a fulfilling and successful career path.

Chapter Eight

Internships are an excellent opportunity for practical experience and new marketable skills in today's competitive job market. On the other side, they can be extremely demanding at times. It would help if you made the most of your internship experience by exercising flexibility wherever possible. Suppose you can adjust to diverse circumstances and rise to new challenges. In that case, you will be able to get the most out of your internship and leave a favorable impression on those who supervise you. The following are five tips that can help you maintain a flexible mentality while participating in an internship, allowing you to get the most out of the experience you are gaining.

- Be conscious of the fact that everything is susceptible to transformation.

When you start working as an intern, you will quickly realize this, mainly because things are constantly changing. Keeping a flexible mindset, being open to new experiences, and taking advantage of new chances is essential. When a project does not turn out as expected, you may be assigned responsibilities that were not a part of the initial plan, or you may be asked to make a sudden shift in how you approach the task. Both of these scenarios are possible. You will be able to get the most out of your internship experience if you recognize that events such as this are a regular part of the job and change your behavior accordingly. This will allow you to make the most of the opportunities presented to you throughout your internship.

When unexpected changes arise, make it a habit to stop and think about how you might transform them into learning opportunities, and then act on your thoughts as soon as possible. It's possible that someone asked you to carry out a duty associated with something you were unfamiliar with or that gives you a chance to hone a skill you've recently acquired. You will learn more helpful information during your internship if you adopt the perspective that you should consider change as an opportunity rather than a challenge. This is because you will be more open to new experiences.

It will help if you remember that some alterations are not under your control. Even while it is doubtful that you could altogether avoid them, it is still possible to adjust to them in a way that is to your advantage. Find ways to turn a shift into an opportunity to learn something new or to challenge yourself rather than allowing it to make you feel frustrated or overburdened, and you'll be better able to deal with the effects of the change.

You will profit in the short term by being adaptive while completing your internship, and you will also be better prepared for the problems you may experience when you enter the actual world of employment in the future.

- Have an open mind.

Maintaining an open mind throughout the internship application and placement process is one of the most critical factors that can lead to a positive outcome. When you start an internship, you should go into it with an open mind, ready to pick up new skills and tackle jobs in a manner that is different from how you may have done them in the past. If you don't go into an internship with an open mind, you won't get the most out of it.

Throughout your internship, keeping an open mind will assist you in being more adaptable and flexible and more prepared for any changes that may arise. If you are willing to let go of the way things have always been done in the past and be open to new ways of doing things, you will be able to get the most out of your experience.

Avoiding making assumptions about how things should be done or how they are "supposed" to be done is a second beneficial method. Time savings could be substantial if this is implemented.

Instead, approach each job with curiosity and an open mind. If you believe thinking outside the box is advantageous, do it. Being open-minded enables you to study a topic from various viewpoints and discover imaginative solutions, which may result in your work having a more substantial influence. Being open-minded also allows you to avoid making snap judgements. If you go into your internship with an open mind, you will learn new things and acquire valuable skills that could help you succeed. If you do this, you will increase your chances of success.

- Do not be afraid to share your opinions with others; their hearing them is something that others value. Because this is one of the most critical pieces of guidance for a successful internship experience, you should not hesitate to communicate your thoughts and opinions with the others involved. In your capacity as an intern, you have a lot to offer both the company you're working with and the team you're a part of. Do not let fear prevent you from sharing your opinions and thoughts with those with power over the current predicament. It would be beneficial if you carried out these actions that exhibited sensitivity and regard for the other person.

When discussing your perspective with others, you should do your best to back it up with facts, data, or research wherever possible. If you have any questions or concerns, you should communicate them appropriately. If you do have questions or concerns, you should speak to them. This will demonstrate that you are involved and enthusiastic in the job that you are doing, which can assist you in creating a favorable connection with both your direct superiors and your coworkers. In addition, this will demonstrate that you are involved and enthusiastic about the work that you are doing.

Remember that your skills and capabilities may go unrecognized if you choose not to speak up when necessary. It would be easier for everyone involved if you had confidence in your abilities and didn't hold back from saying what's on your mind.

- Be on the lookout for opportunities; consider signing up for a summer internship to gain and expand your skills. If you believe that taking on more tasks or projects will assist you in further developing your talents, do not be afraid to request those opportunities.

Many employers are willing to provide their interns with more challenging work to perform during their time with them if they are asked to do so. Imagine if the company you currently work for does not provide any more opportunities for advancement.

Suppose you do not have any luck there. In that case, you may want to explore looking into other organizations or volunteer opportunities in your sector that may be able to provide you with the additional experience you require. In this instance, you may consider looking into other organizations or volunteer opportunities in your industry. Attending professional events, such as conferences, seminars, or networking events, can provide you with the necessary connections that could lead to new opportunities.

Attending events of this nature at which professionals congregate might also assist you in expanding your professional network. In conclusion, you should make the most of any resources that are made available to you by your firm to further increase both your capabilities and your knowledge base. If you are willing to put in some work and demonstrate some initiative during your internship, you will be able to get the most out of the experience you are obtaining from the position.

- Keep an upbeat attitude at all times.

During your internship, you must be adaptable and open to new experiences. Thus, having a positive attitude is crucial.

It is normal to feel frustrated when things don't go as planned; nonetheless, it is necessary to maintain a positive attitude and be open to new ideas in these situations. Keeping a positive outlook will help you feel better about yourself and make it easier to deal with unforeseen changes. Nevertheless, it will indicate to potential employers that you can handle anything that comes your way. In addition, it is crucial to maintain a good attitude regarding the obligations delegated to you, even if they differ from what you had first intended or fall outside your expectations.

In addition, keeping a healthy outlook on one's abilities is critical. Don't be too hard on yourself if things don't go as planned; use it as a learning lesson. Being flexible implies being willing to take risks, accept that you may be wrong, and develop due to the lessons you've learned. Maintaining a constructive outlook can assist you in keeping an open mind regarding the myriad of new opportunities and experiences that may come your way.

Remember that having a good attitude is one of the finest ways to set yourself apart from the other individuals in your group since it demonstrates that you care about what others think. If you already possess this quality, you can put it to good use during your internship as it is in such high demand among potential employers.

Chapter Nine

Your Training Plan and Intern Responsibilities: Guiding the Course of Your Internship

An internship presents an unparalleled opportunity to gain hands-on experience, build a professional network, and potentially kickstart your career. Central to this process are your training plan and intern responsibilities—two critical elements broadly defining your internship experience. Understanding, navigating, and leveraging these factors will ensure you maximize your time as an intern. This chapter serves as your guide to effectively deal with these components and take a step forward toward your professional aspirations.

Understanding Your Training Plan

- A training plan is your roadmap for the duration of the internship. It outlines the skills and knowledge you'll acquire, the tasks you undertake, and the goals you're expected to achieve. Your training plan may be broadly divided into phases, starting with orientation, moving on to specific skill training, then task implementation, and concluding with an evaluation.

- Orientation Phase: This phase typically involves introducing you to the company, its culture, its operations, and the team you'll work with. It provides a broad overview of what you can expect during your internship.

- Skill Training Phase: You'll receive training on specific skills pertinent to your role. For example, if you're in a marketing internship, you may be trained in market research, content creation, or digital marketing tools.

- Task Implementation Phase: Armed with your new skills, you'll be given tasks to apply your learning. This could range from assisting in ongoing projects to potentially leading a small project of your own.

- Evaluation Phase: Toward the end of your internship, there will usually be an evaluation of your performance, assessing the progress you've made, the skills you've developed, and the areas where you might need further improvement.

Navigating Your Intern Responsibilities

The specific responsibilities you'll shoulder as an intern can significantly vary depending on the company, the industry, and your role. However, some everyday responsibilities across most internships include:

- Assisting in Projects: Most of your time as an intern will likely be spent helping in ongoing projects. This will allow you to apply your skills in a real-world setting and understand how different parts of the organization come together to complete a task.

- Performing Administrative Tasks: Interns are often tasked with administrative duties such as scheduling meetings, maintaining records, or managing databases. These tasks, while seeming mundane, are integral to organizational operations and can offer insights into the company's workings.
- Conducting Research: Interns are commonly tasked with researching to assist in decision-making. This could involve market research, competitor analysis, or investigating industry trends.
- Presenting Findings: You may also be responsible for presenting your work or research findings to your team or supervisor. This is an excellent opportunity to develop your communication and presentation skills.

Making the Most of Your Training Plan and Responsibilities

Embrace Learning: Take every task as an opportunity to learn something new. Even the most menial tasks can teach you about the organization, the industry, and how to navigate the workplace.

Ask Questions: Don't hesitate to ask if you're unsure about anything. It's better to seek clarification than to make uninformed mistakes.

Be Proactive: Take initiative where you can. Proactively proposing a new idea, volunteering for a task, or simply helping a colleague can make a positive impression.

Network: Networking is a crucial part of any internship. Build relationships with your colleagues and supervisors. You never know who might provide you with a valuable opportunity.

Seek Feedback: Regularly seek feedback on your performance. It will help you understand where you excel and where you need to improve.

Reflect: Take time weekly to reflect on what you've learned and accomplished. This will help you track your progress and plan your next steps.

In conclusion, your training plan and intern responsibilities guide your internship journey. Embracing and leveraging them effectively can make your internship an enriching experience. Remember, the key to a successful internship is a positive attitude, a willingness to learn, and the initiative to maximize every opportunity.

Chapter Ten

Harnessing Distinctive Opportunities: Workplace and Company Culture

Every company and workplace is unique, boasting its distinct character and spirit. This unique blend of values, traditions, beliefs, interactions, and behaviors, collectively called 'company culture', shapes the organization's soul. An inviting and engaging company culture nurtures an encouraging environment and offers exceptional personal and professional growth opportunities. This chapter aims to delve into these opportunities and guide you on capitalizing on them for your career development.

Understanding Company Culture

Before we explore the opportunities a company's culture can present— it's crucial to understand what it means. A company's culture can be likened to an individual's personality. It encapsulates the company's work environment, values, ethics, expectations, goals, and mission. It significantly influences how employees, management, and stakeholders interact with each other and how they perceive the company.

The company culture is often communicated through its mission statement, goals, and practices, but it truly comes alive through its people's everyday actions, behaviors, and decisions. It's important to remember that a positive company culture promotes employee satisfaction, productivity, and retention while enhancing its reputation.

The Opportunities Presented by a Positive Company Culture

- **Learning and Development:**

A company with a culture that values learning and development encourages employees to upskill and expand their knowledge base. It may offer training programs, mentorship opportunities, and access to industry events or resources. Leveraging these opportunities allows you to grow professionally and stay competitive.

- **Networking:**

Companies that foster a collaborative culture provide ample networking opportunities. By working on team projects, participating in company events, or joining company-supported professional groups, you can build valuable relationships that can propel your career forward.

- **Leadership Opportunities:**

A company culture that encourages initiative and innovation often provides opportunities for employees to take on leadership roles. These can come as leading a project, mentoring a junior team member, or initiating a new process or project.

- **Recognition and Rewards:**

Companies with cultures that value recognition tend to have systems to reward their employees' hard work. These could be in the form of promotions, bonuses, or recognition programs. These provide a morale boost and tangible benefits that can help advance your career.

- **Employee Wellness:**

Organizations that highly value employee well-being often provide resources and opportunities to promote mental and physical health. These can include wellness programs, flexible work schedules, and mental health resources. These opportunities can significantly improve your work-life balance and overall job satisfaction.

Understanding and Aligning With Your Company's Culture

To capitalize on the opportunities your company's culture presents, you must first understand that culture. Take the time to observe and ask questions about the company's values, practices, and traditions. Look at how people interact with each other, how decisions are made, and how work is done.

Once you understand the company's culture well, seek to align yourself with it. This doesn't mean losing your unique identity or unthinkingly conforming. Instead, it's about balancing your values and the company's. When your values align with your company's, you are more likely to be satisfied with your work, perform better, and seize the opportunities the company culture presents.

In conclusion, a company's culture provides many personal and professional growth opportunities. By understanding and aligning yourself with your company's culture, you can capitalize on these opportunities and propel your career forward. Remember, it's not just about fitting into a company's culture; it's about leveraging that culture for growth, development, and career success.

Chapter Eleven

As the saying goes, "Smooth seas do not make skillful sailors." As you navigate the vast ocean of your professional life, you will inevitably encounter some turbulent waters. It's during these times of adversity that your true mettle is tested. Whether managing setbacks, resolving conflicts, handling stress, or maintaining a work-life balance, overcoming challenges is crucial to professional growth. This chapter thoroughly explores these elements, guiding you toward building resilience and cultivating a positive mindset.

- **Dealing with Setbacks and Difficult Situations**

Setbacks are an integral part of any professional journey. Whether a rejected proposal, a lost client, or a project failure, setbacks can feel like a significant blow. However, viewing these not as failures but as learning opportunities is essential.

Firstly, it's essential to allow yourself to feel disappointed. It's a natural reaction to setbacks; acknowledging these feelings is part of the healing process. Then, adopt a problem-solving approach. Analyze what went wrong and why. What could have been done differently? How can this inform your future actions?

Let's consider an example. Imagine you're a marketing intern, and your campaign proposal is rejected. You might initially feel disheartened. But instead of dwelling on the rejection, try to understand its reasons. Seek feedback from your supervisor, and use it constructively to improve your future proposals.

- **Conflict Resolution and Effective Problem-Solving**

Conflicts are unavoidable in a professional setting. Diverse personalities, conflicting interests, and high-pressure environments can sometimes lead to misunderstandings and disputes.

The key to effective conflict resolution is open, respectful communication. Begin by trying to understand the other person's point of view. What are their concerns? How are they feeling? Address the issue at hand, not the person. Be assertive yet respectful.

Problem-solving is another crucial skill. Begin by clearly defining the problem. Then, brainstorm possible solutions. Evaluate the pros and cons of each, and choose the most viable option. Implement it, and monitor the results, making changes if necessary.

Let's say, you're part of a team working on a project, and there's disagreement over the strategy to be followed. You could address this by organizing a meeting, allowing everyone to express their views, and collectively brainstorming a solution. This not only resolves the conflict but also fosters a sense of teamwork.

Case Study: Conflict Resolution and Effective Problem-Solving

Background

Anika worked as a project manager at a dynamic digital marketing firm. She was renowned for her strategic thinking and communication skills, leading a diverse team of creative professionals. While often producing impressive results, the collaboration of varied personalities and perspectives occasionally led to conflicts and disagreements.

Challenge

A particular project that Anika was leading involved a campaign for a significant client. A dispute arose within her team regarding the creative direction of the movement. Two key team members had strongly contrasting views and were reluctant to compromise. The ongoing disagreement delayed the project and created a tense atmosphere within the team.

The Journey to Conflict Resolution and Effective Problem-Solving

Step 1: Acknowledging the Conflict

Anika's first step was acknowledging the conflict openly instead of avoiding it. She called for a team meeting to discuss the issue, providing a platform where everyone could express their thoughts and feelings openly.

Step 2: Understanding Different Perspectives

In the meeting, Anika encouraged both parties to explain their viewpoints clearly. She made sure to foster an atmosphere of respect and open communication. This enabled everyone in the team to understand the different perspectives and where each person came from.

Step 3: Identifying the Root Cause

With the perspectives on the table, Anika guided the team to identify the underlying cause of the disagreement. It was a difference in understanding the client's requirements, leading to conflicting ideas for the campaign's creative direction.

Step 4: Collaborative Problem-Solving

Once the root cause was identified, Anika initiated a problem-solving session. The team collectively brainstormed ways to align their creative ideas with the client's expectations. She ensured everyone's ideas were heard, promoting an inclusive and cooperative environment.

Step 5: Reaching a Compromise

Through collaborative discussion, the team was able to merge the best parts of both ideas, resulting in a comprehensive campaign strategy that was in line with the client's requirements. Both conflicting parties agreed to this compromise, resolving the conflict.

Step 6: Implementing Conflict Management Strategies

To prevent such conflicts in the future, Anika implemented conflict management strategies within her team. She introduced regular team meetings for open communication, a straightforward process for decision-making, and training sessions for conflict resolution and effective communication.

Outcome

The resolution of the conflict led to a more harmonious work environment. The team completed the campaign successfully, resulting in a satisfied client. The strategies implemented by Anika also led to improved communication within the group, helping prevent similar conflicts in the future.

Conclusion

Anika's case study highlights the importance of effective conflict resolution and problem-solving in a professional environment. Her approach—acknowledging the conflict, understanding different perspectives, identifying the root cause, collaborative problem-solving, reaching a compromise, and implementing conflict management strategies—is a practical roadmap for managing workplace disputes. It showcases that conflicts can lead to better understanding, improved communication, and enhanced team performance when handled effectively.

- **Managing Stress and Maintaining Work-Life Balance**

Balancing your work responsibilities and personal life can seem like a tightrope as a professional. Add to that the stress of meeting deadlines, handling pressure, and striving to excel, which can sometimes become overwhelming.

Stress management is a crucial skill to master. This could involve activities like meditation, exercise, or pursuing a hobby. Remember, taking regular breaks and giving yourself time to relax and rejuvenate is essential.

Similarly, maintaining a work-life balance is not about a precisely equal division of time but about achieving a fulfilling equilibrium between your professional and personal life. It's essential to set boundaries and learn to say no when necessary.

If you find that work is taking up all your time, leaving you drained and without time for yourself or your family, it might be time to reevaluate. Could some tasks be delegated? Are you taking on more than you can handle? Are you able to disconnect from work during your time?

Case Study: Managing Stress and Maintaining Work-Life Balance

Background

John, a hard-working IT professional, was well-known in his company for his dedication and commitment to work. His technical expertise and problem-solving abilities were admired by colleagues and superiors alike. However, as his job demands grew, John became increasingly engulfed in a swirl of stress and mounting work pressures.

Challenge

John's job involved managing critical systems and troubleshooting urgent issues, often requiring him to work late hours. The line between his professional and personal life began to blur. His stress levels skyrocketed, his health deteriorated, and his relationships suffered. John realized he needed to manage his stress and establish a work-life balance.

The Journey to Stress Management and Work-Life Balance

Step 1: Acknowledging the Problem

The first step in John's journey was acknowledging that he was stressed and that his work-life balance was skewed. He recognized that his relentless focus on work was not sustainable and was taking a toll on his overall well-being.

Step 2: Identifying Stressors and Boundaries

John made a list of the elements of his job that were causing him the most stress. He also identified when his work infringed on his personal life. This exercise helped him realize that he needed to establish more explicit boundaries and find ways to manage his high-stress tasks more effectively.

Step 3: Implementing Stress Management Techniques

John started incorporating stress management techniques into his daily routine. He began with short meditation sessions every morning and lighted physical exercises after work. He also took regular breaks during the workday, stepping away from his desk to clear his mind.

Step 4: Prioritizing and Delegating

John realized he couldn't do everything himself and started prioritizing his tasks. He began delegating tasks where possible and focused on the most critical jobs. This reduced his workload and helped him manage his stress levels.

Step 5: Establishing Work-Life Boundaries

John made it a rule not to bring work home. He committed to disconnecting from work emails and calls during his time. This clear delineation helped him focus on his personal life and interests outside of work.

Step 6: Building a Support Network

John contacted colleagues, friends, and family, sharing his experiences and seeking their support. They provided him comfort, advice, and a fresh perspective on managing work-related stress and maintaining a work-life balance.

Outcome

Over the ensuing months, John felt a significant reduction in his stress levels. He found himself more energized, both at work and home. His performance at work remained high, and his relationships improved. Despite the demands of his job, he successfully carved out time for himself, achieving a healthier work-life balance.

Conclusion

John's case study offers an insightful view into workplace stress and the importance of maintaining a work-life balance. It underlines that recognizing stressors, implementing stress management techniques, prioritizing tasks, establishing clear work-life boundaries, and seeking support are crucial to combat stress and achieving a healthy work-life equilibrium. John's journey is an encouraging testament that, with mindful adjustments, it is possible to manage stress effectively and lead a balanced life.

• Building Resilience and a Positive Mindset

Resilience is the ability to bounce back from adversity. It's about having the mental fortitude to withstand hardships and continue marching forward. This cannot be achieved overnight but is developed through experiences and conscious effort.

Building a positive mindset is a crucial aspect of resilience. This involves viewing challenges as opportunities for growth rather than insurmountable obstacles. It's about believing in your capabilities and maintaining a positive outlook, even in difficult circumstances.

Surround yourself with positive influences, whether people, books, or experiences. Practice self-care and remember to celebrate your victories, however small. Adapt to changing circumstances and be open to new experiences and opportunities.

In conclusion, the road to professional success is riddled with challenges and adversities. However, these can be transformed into stepping stones to growth and achievement with the right mindset and tools. Remember, the most significant challenges often lead to the greatest triumphs. So, face these challenges head-on, learn from your setbacks, resolve conflicts effectively, manage your stress, maintain a work-life balance, build resilience and foster a positive mindset.

Now that you've gathered insights into overcoming challenges and adversity, you're ready to embark on the next step of your professional journey: transitioning from internship to career. But before you proceed, why not explore some more resources on www.inspireambitions.com? You'll find practical advice and tools for personal growth and career progression here. Remember, every challenge is an opportunity in disguise, and you can turn every setback into a comeback. So go forth and conquer!

Case Study: Building Resilience and a Positive Mindset

Background

Meet Sarah. She was a fresh graduate from university, excited to embark on her professional journey. With a degree in marketing, she secured an internship at a leading advertising firm. The world was her oyster, but she soon realized that the professional world was more challenging than she had imagined.

Challenge

Sarah was entrusted with significant tasks within the first few months of her internship. She was excited but also felt a great deal of pressure. Despite her best efforts, a campaign she developed did not perform well during one project. The client was disappointed, and Sarah was devastated. This setback, combined with the rigorous demands of her job, began to affect her mental health. She felt overwhelmed and was slipping into a negative mindset.

The Journey to Resilience and Positivity

Step 1: Acknowledging the Setback

The first step in Sarah's journey was acknowledging her feelings. She recognized that she was disappointed and overwhelmed. Instead of repressing these emotions, she accepted them as a natural response.

Step 2: Seeking Support

Sarah understood that she needed help. She reached out to her mentor at work, sharing her feelings and concerns. Her mentor reminded her that setbacks were part of the learning process and encouraged her not to be too hard on herself.

Step 3: Reflection and Learning

Sarah took a step back and reflected on the failed campaign. She sought feedback, identified areas where she could have done better, and noted these as key learning points for future projects.

Step 4: Self-care and Stress Management

Recognizing the toll that stress was taking on her, Sarah took up yoga and started setting aside time each day for relaxation and rejuvenation. She made a point of disconnecting from work during these times, allowing herself the space to recover and recharge.

Step 5: Building a Positive Mindset

Sarah began to cultivate a positive mindset consciously. She started a gratitude journal, noting daily positive experiences and things she was grateful for. This practice helped her focus on the positives in her life, boosting her morale.

Step 6: Embracing Failure as a Learning Opportunity

With time, Sarah began to view failures not as catastrophes but as opportunities to learn and grow. She recognized that each setback added to her experience and honed her skills.

Outcome

Over the next few months during her internship, Sarah saw a significant transformation in herself. She was not only handling stress better but was also more resilient. She faced challenges head-on, learning from each experience. When another of her campaigns underperformed, she took it in stride, using it as a learning opportunity rather than letting it dampen her spirits.

Conclusion

Sarah's journey is an inspirational case study for building resilience and cultivating a positive mindset. It highlights the importance of acknowledging setbacks, seeking support, self-care, and viewing challenges as opportunities for growth. Most importantly, it underscores the reality that resilience and positivity are not inherent traits but skills that can be developed with conscious effort and persistence. So, let's take a leaf out of Sarah's book and start building our resilience today!

Chapter Twelve

The conclusion of your internship period represents turning a pivotal page in your career journey. The exhilarating shift from intern to full-time employee is an exciting but equally challenging endeavor. But fret not. This transition can be successfully navigated by implementing a four-fold strategy: evaluate, showcase, secure, and prepare. Let's dive into this.

1. Evaluating Your Internship Experience and Lessons Learned.

As you bid farewell to your internship, reflecting upon the entire experience is paramount. Probe into the details of your learning journey. For instance, if you were an intern at a software firm, did you learn a new programming language? Or perhaps, you have sharpened your problem-solving abilities by working on complex codes.

Similarly, suppose you interned in a marketing role. In that case, you might have gained insights into consumer behavior, honed your creativity by participating in campaign brainstorming sessions, or learned digital marketing tools. Every project you undertook, every challenge you overcame, and every interaction you engaged in has added something to your professional persona. Document these learnings as they will form the bedrock of your career progression.

2. Showcasing Your Internship Experience on Your CV and During Interviews.

Think of your CV as your professional autobiography and an exhibition of your capabilities. Under the 'Work Experience' section, chronicle your internship journey. Outline your role, responsibilities, and, most importantly, your achievements. Let's say you interned in a financial firm and streamlined a process that reduced time spent on a task by 20%. This information becomes a crucial element of your CV.

In the context of interviews, your internship experience becomes a storybook filled with real-life examples demonstrating your skills. For instance, when questioned about your problem-solving abilities, you could recount when you resolved a software glitch during a project's crucial stage, preventing potential delays.

3. Securing References and Recommendations.

A reference from your supervisor or a recommendation from a colleague can be a potent tool in your job-seeking arsenal. Suppose you had a supportive supervisor who appreciated your work during your internship. In that case, they could provide a glowing reference or LinkedIn recommendation that solidifies your professional credibility.

Remember, these gestures are two-way streets. Offer to endorse their skills on LinkedIn and express gratitude for their support during your internship. This not only secures your references but also strengthens your professional network.

4. Preparing for the Transition from Intern to Full-Time Employee

Transitioning from an intern to a full-time employee is like switching from a small pond to a vast lake. The responsibilities increase, the expectations soar, and the room for errors diminishes.

The earlier relatively lenient deadlines could be replaced with stringent timelines. The work hours may increase, and the learning curve could become steeper. For example, you might have contributed campaign ideas as a marketing intern. Still, as a full-time employee, you could be entrusted with planning and executing them.

Alongside your work responsibilities, cultivate your professional image. Dress appropriately, exhibit punctuality, show initiative, and always communicate courteously and respectfully. These small yet impactful habits reflect your professionalism and commitment.

The shift from an intern to a full-time professional isn't just a change in your job title; it's an evolution in your professional journey. It's an exciting phase of self-discovery, learning, and growth. And remember, each day is a new opportunity to learn and excel.

For more career progression, professional development, and personal growth resources, visit my blog at www.inspireambitions.com. It is packed with helpful resources from CV templates.

Chapter Thirteen
Paving the Way for Your Future

An internship can be an enriching and transformative experience, offering a taste of the professional world, providing growth opportunities, and serving as a stepping stone for your career. However, the journey doesn't end when your internship does. The steps you take post-internship can profoundly influence the trajectory of your professional path. This chapter will guide you through these critical steps, ensuring you fully capitalize on your internship experience.

Reflect on Your Experience

Your first step after the internship should be to reflect on your experience. Ask yourself:

What did I learn from this internship? What new skills and knowledge did I gain?

How have I grown personally and professionally?

What did I enjoy about my work, and what did I dislike?

Did my internship experience align with my career aspirations?

What feedback did I receive, and how can I use it for my growth?

Your answers to these questions will provide valuable insights to guide your career decisions and help you strategize your next steps.

Update Your CV and Portfolio

Once you have reflected on your experience, update your CV and portfolio with your internship experience. Highlight the skills you've gained, the projects you've worked on, and the responsibilities you've shouldered. Remember, potential employers are interested in the results you've achieved, your impact, and the value you can bring to their organization.

Request a Letter of Recommendation

If you have built a positive relationship with your supervisor or any senior organization member, consider asking them for a letter of recommendation. Such a letter can bolster your applications for future jobs or academic pursuits. Be sure to request the letter well before you need it and provide the person writing it with all the necessary details, such as your accomplishments and contributions during your internship.

Maintain Your Professional Relationships

The professional relationships you've formed during your internship are invaluable. Ensure to maintain these relationships even after your internship ends. Connect with your colleagues and superiors on professional networking platforms like LinkedIn, and keep them updated about your career progress. These connections can provide career advice, job opportunities, and references to benefit your career journey.

Plan Your Next Steps

Based on your internship experience and reflection, plan your next steps. If your internship confirmed your career aspirations, you might want to seek similar roles or continue your education. If it made you realize that the field wasn't the right fit for you, consider exploring other sectors or functions. Remember, there's no one-size-fits-all career path, and exploring and experimenting to find what truly fulfills you is okay.

Keep Learning

Never stop learning. Whether it's a new skill, a new field, or a deeper dive into your chosen sector, continual learning will keep you adaptable, relevant, and competitive in today's rapidly evolving job market. Consider enrolling in courses, attending workshops, or gaining certifications to enhance your skill set and make you more attractive to potential employers.

In conclusion, your post-internship steps can shape your career trajectory. You can navigate your career path by reflecting on your experience, updating your CV and portfolio, securing a letter of recommendation, maintaining your professional relationships, planning your next steps, and continuing to learn.

Remember, every experience, whether positive or negative, offers lessons and growth opportunities. Make the most of them, and you'll be well-equipped to tackle the challenges and seize the opportunities that come your way in your professional journey.

The Launchpad for Future Success

It's been quite a journey. You've traversed the initial stages of understanding the job market, sought out an internship that aligns with your career objectives, navigated the recruitment process, and worked hard to make a meaningful impact during your time as an intern. By now, you've learned a great deal, accumulated new skills, and forged invaluable relationships. In this closing chapter, we will reflect on this journey and draw out the key takeaways, offering practical advice for your ongoing career development.

1. Reflect on your Internship Experience

The end of an internship should not mean the end of your learning curve. On the contrary, it is the perfect time to pause and reflect on the invaluable experience you've gained. What were your significant achievements and challenges? Which skills did you enhance, and which new ones did you acquire? A reflection is a powerful tool for self-awareness and personal development, so pen down these reflections in a journal or an online document.

2. Continual Skill Development

Your learning must not end here. Every new experience, every project, and every person you interact with can teach you something new. Take ownership of your development. Keep updating your skills, explore new fields, and always stay curious. The world is in continuous flux, especially in the face of technological advancements, so keeping your skills relevant and up-to-date is critical.

- **Build and Maintain Networks**

Remember that the professional relationships you forged during your internship are crucial to your career development. Stay in touch with your colleagues, superiors, and mentors. Social networking platforms like LinkedIn can be beneficial in this regard. The connections you've made today can open up many opportunities tomorrow.

- **Be Proactive**

The professional world appreciates proactive individuals who take charge of their careers. Don't wait for opportunities to come knocking on your door. Seek them out. Research companies you would like to work for, contact professionals in your field of interest, and attend industry events.

- **Set Your Goals and Review Them**

Setting career goals is an ongoing process. Now that you have experienced the working world reassess your objectives. What did you enjoy about your internship? What didn't you like? Use these experiences to set new goals or to tweak your existing ones. And remember, it's okay to change your mind along the way. Life is not static, and neither are your career goals.

I invite you to visit my blog at www.inspireambitions.com. It offers a treasure trove of resources to guide your career journey. It has everything you need, from templates for resumes and cover letters to goal-setting resources and interview tips.

If you want to dig deeper and continue on this journey of professional and personal development, here is another resource website for you;

https://inspireambitions.com/career-hub/

And remember, your internship is just one small step in your journey, a launchpad toward a successful future. It's where you've learned to convert theories into practice, where you've made mistakes and grown from them. So, carry these experiences and lessons with you as you move from your campus to your career, and you'll build a future that is not just successful but also fulfilling.

On this note, I leave you to continue your journey, equipped with the insights and tools needed to navigate the fascinating world of professional life. And always remember: You are capable, you are adaptable, and you are ready to make your mark. It's time to launch!

Bonus Chapter

In this transforming chapter, we look into a critical part of your professional life: the power of recognizing and maximizing the value of your current employment. This is a crucial aspect of your professional life since it may significantly impact your career. It is pretty simple to become preoccupied with the search for better opportunities and lose sight of the great potential already in your current employment. Not only will you contribute to developing a pleasant working environment, but you will also be laying the groundwork for your future success in doing your job with the highest seriousness, absolute dedication, and constant pursuit of perfection. This chapter is meant to serve as a personal reminder to appreciate and flourish in your current position, keeping in mind that doing so can lead to even more significant opportunities in the future.

Recognizing the Gravity of the Unemployment Problem

Before we delve into the topic of how important it is to appreciate the work you already have, it is essential first to realize the unpleasant reality of being unemployed. Being unemployed may be a mentally and emotionally taxing situation for people. The pressure on one's finances, the loss of their purpose in life, and the effect on one's self-esteem can all contribute to a profound sense of hopelessness. We understand why making the most of your current employment is necessary and a privilege when we acknowledge the seriousness of the issue we are currently confronted with.

The Power of Appreciation

Your current position already provides you with several opportunities. It offers security, a source of money, and a platform on which to develop skills and experience that are valuable in their own right. It is of the utmost importance to be grateful for the present and aware of the opportunities it presents for personal and professional development. You may establish a positive framework that can lead to improved performance and a more enjoyable experience at work by transforming your perspective to one of appreciation.

Building a Stellar Reputation

Your professional reputation is essential, notwithstanding your job title or the field in which you work. Building a solid track record and establishing yourself as a professional who can be counted on requires you to give your current position the serious attention it deserves and produce excellent outcomes. It is essential to remember that your reputation will often precede you, which will open doors to chances in the future that otherwise might not have been available. In this session, we will discuss tactics that may be used to build a fantastic reputation for yourself and establish yourself as a member of your organization who is trusted and valued.

Developing Transferable Skills

Every work presents its own particular set of difficulties and possibilities for professional growth. You can develop valuable skills and knowledge that will serve you well in future endeavors if you devote your full attention and effort to the responsibilities of your current work. It is crucial to seize opportunities for advancement, take on new responsibilities, learn from colleagues, and consistently enhance the skill set that you already possess. The acquired knowledge can serve as a stepping stone toward attaining possibilities that are even more desirable in the future. In this session, we will examine productive tactics for locating and capitalizing on options for advancement within your current position at work.

Developing a Growth Mindset

It is essential to your long-term success to approach the job you are now working for with a growth mentality. The vital components of adopting this mindset are showing a willingness to take on difficulties, actively seeking feedback, and working to improve continuously. When you have a growth mindset, you foster an atmosphere that is resilient, adaptable, and open to learning throughout your life. These characteristics will serve you well no matter what path you choose in your professional life. In the context of your current job, we will discuss concrete methods for fostering a development mindset and promoting a growth mindset in others.

Establishing Connections and Working the Network

Your current position offers a fantastic platform to create professional relationships and engage in networking activities. Building relationships with coworkers, bosses, and others in your field can significantly impact your career's direction. Steps vital to creating lasting professional relationships include participating in activities geared toward networking and collaboration, working with others on projects, and making constructive contributions to a positive and encouraging work culture. During this session, we will talk about successful networking strategies and techniques for creating relationships, both of which can assist you in expanding your professional network and opening doors to new opportunities.

The Influence of Being Thankful

Your general sense of well-being and enjoyment from your work can be significantly improved by cultivating gratitude toward your current position. Creating an environment of appreciation that elevates your spirits and pushes you to perform at your best can be accomplished by setting aside time each day to think about the gratifying elements of your job, the abilities you are refining, and the development you are experiencing. In this session, we will investigate the transforming power of thankfulness and examine some practical activities for building a sense of appreciation and fulfillment within your current line of work.

Conclusion

It would help if you never undervalued the importance of appreciating and succeeding in the work that you now hold as you move on in your professional life. The building blocks of a professionally satisfying and fruitful life are an appreciation for the opportunities it provides, an openness to the challenges it confronts, and a never-ending pursuit of development.

Giving your absolute best effort in the position you already hold not only boosts your professional reputation but also paves the way for even more significant accomplishments in the years to come. Therefore, recognize the significance of gratitude, make the most of your current position's opportunities, and watch as your perseverance and determination propel you toward a future rich in prosperity, advancement, and accomplishment.

Overcoming Boredom and Discovering the Positive in Your Work

In this energizing chapter, we look into the typical difficulty of feeling bored and stagnant in your work, whether in a new position or a role you've been in for a while. This challenge is expected whether you're in a part you've been in for a time or a position you've been in for a while. In this session, we will discuss ways to prevent slipping into boredom and learn how to consistently find positivity and enthusiasm in your professional life. You can revolutionize your working experience and unlock your full potential if you commit to active participation and strive to maintain a reasonable frame of mind.

Recognizing the Boredom Trap is the First Section

Boredom can affect everyone, regardless of their job title or the field in which they work. It frequently presents itself as a lack of drive, apathy, or a sense of repetition in the daily activities that you engage in. Identifying the symptoms of boredom is the first step in finding a solution to the problem.

You may notice that you are executing activities mechanistically, that your productivity is falling, or that you are experiencing general unhappiness. You can actively recover your enthusiasm and reignite your passion for your profession if you first acknowledge and then address the sentiments preventing you from doing so.

Having a Growth Mindset

A growth mindset is a great skill that can help you overcome boredom and find fulfillment in your work—believing that your capabilities and abilities may be improved via hard work and dedication is a necessary component of this mindset. When you have a growth mentality, you consider difficulties as chances for personal development and professional advancement. You develop a greater willingness to try new things, actively seek criticism, and continually seek improvement. This shift in perspective enables you to approach each day with a sense of curiosity and a desire to push your boundaries, allowing you to find excitement in growing and developing yourself.

Seeking Out Fresh Obstacles

Seeking out new challenges to take on inside your current position is an efficient strategy for warding off feelings of boredom. Look for possibilities to take on more responsibility or participate in endeavors that will force you to step beyond your comfort zone. Volunteering in activities or projects that share your interests but may need you to learn new skills can be very rewarding. You may maintain the vitality and excitement of your career by constantly searching out new challenges. Avoiding monotony is just one of the many benefits that may be gained through actively seeking out new challenges and opportunities for personal and professional development.

Embracing Lifelong Learning

Learning is a process that continues throughout one's life, and adopting a mentality that encourages ongoing education can infuse one's work with energy and zeal. Keep an eye out for learning opportunities so that you can hone your expertise. Participate in relevant professional development activities such as workshops, seminars, or industry conferences. Pursue professional development classes or credentials.

Participate in self-directed education through reading books, listening to podcasts, or consulting online resources. You can avoid boredom in your work-life by consistently prioritizing engaging in your personal development. This will allow you to become aware of new areas of interest, enable you to remain current with developments in your business, and prevent you from falling behind.

Building Meaningful Relationships

Constructing meaningful connections with one's coworkers and one's superiors can be an effective treatment for boredom in the office. Your working environment can benefit from a surge of revitalized energy if you try to cultivate connections with coworkers and encourage a sense of camaraderie among them. It would help if you looked for opportunities to work together on projects, participate in events that form teams, or contribute to efforts across departments. You might want to look into hiring a mentor who can assist you in navigating your professional journey by providing direction and assistance. You may develop a supportive network that supports growth, ignites creativity, and helps you find renewed joy in your work by cultivating meaningful relationships.

Embracing Creative and Innovative Thinking

Even the most mundane responsibilities can be given a new lease on life by injecting creativity and originality into one's work. Put yourself to the test by trying new ways of thinking and coming up with original concepts. You should try new methods and procedures to complete your work more originally or efficiently. Investigate how your existing function might be enhanced through innovation and development. If you allow yourself to be creative, you can turn boring jobs into exciting opportunities for experimenting and discovering new things, preventing boredom from setting in.

Putting Gratitude and Positive Thinking

Finding the good in your work, no matter how insignificant it may seem, can significantly impact the happiness you experience overall. Gratitude can be practiced by recognizing and appreciating the possibilities and blessings that come your way due to your job. Pay attention to the parts of your job that you particularly like or that fulfill you. Honor one another's successes, no matter how large or small. Make a mental shift to positivity and optimism, recasting difficulties as opportunities for personal development, and focus on taking action.

You'll be able to navigate through difficult times with fortitude and find renewed energy and passion if you actively seek out the positive aspects of your profession and cultivate a positive mindset.

Conclusion

Boredom in the workplace is a typical problem, but it can be overcome using the appropriate tactics and mentality. You can infuse your work with passion and purpose if you know the warning signs of boredom, adopt a growth mindset, seek out new challenges, develop relationships, embrace creativity and innovation, and regularly practice thankfulness and positivity.

Remember that each new day brings the possibility of advancing your career and discovering new levels of personal satisfaction. Therefore, embrace engagement, seek out new opportunities, and watch as monotony goes away, creating a place for excitement, innovation, and a revitalized love for your work. Your route to a work-life that is meaningful and engaging begins at this very moment.

Printed in the USA
CPSIA information can be obtained
at www.ICGtesting.com
CBHW030841011124
16733CB00023B/658